THE PRODIGAL SON
A Story of Deliverance from Sin

By
Harold J. Simms, Jr.
Xulon Press

Xulon Press
2301 Lucien Way #415
Maitland, FL 32751
407.339.4217
www.xulonpress.com

Printed in the United States of America.

ISBN-13: 9781498475761

About the Author

P astor Harold Simms, Jr. was born on July 29, 1952 in Tacoma WA. He is the oldest child of Pastor Mary and Deacon Harold Simms, Sr. As of this date, Harold Pastor's the God's Pentecostal Church where he had served as a member for 60 years. Before taking the Lead Pastor's position, he served as the Assistant Pastor for sixteen years. God saw fit for him to marry his best friend, Barbara Ann Simms on June 30, 2000. They are the proud parents of two children and seven grandchildren.

Pastor Simms received Christ into his life at the age of 6 years old. He is grateful to the Lord for never leaving him even when he chose to go his own way. Prior to receiving Christ, Pastor Simms chose to practice homosexuality for 15 years, but even in the chose's he made, God still expressed His love and mercy towards him.

In this book he shares the dark life he lived. It's been said that anyone who practices homosexuality is considered to be gay. However, the real definition of the word gay means you are happy and joyful. In Harold's case, he was always very sad in spirit. In this book, he shares the joy of coming out of that dark closet of sin into the light of Christ. Harold is hopeful that through his story, someone will receive Christ into their life. God is a God of love, not hate. Through His love, God has done something very wonderful in Harold's life.

Contents

ACKNOWLEDGMENTS

Special Honor to my Parents, the late
Pastor Mary and Deacon Harold Simms, Sr.
My Sister,
Betty Jane Simms

All Praise and Glory to my Lord and Savior Jesus Christ!

A warm thank-you and acknowledgment to my wife and best friend: Evangelist Barbara Simms and to my supervisor, Mrs. Jackson for their consistent support while on this writing journey.

To my three children, seven grandchildren and extended family – THANK YOU!

Specials thanks to: Pastor Gary Wyatt, Dr. Edna Travis, Dr. Lisa and Brother Reginald Macklin, Overseer Greg and DeCarlo Jackson, President Helen Smith, Bishop Lois Sharpe, and the late Evangelist Joann Davis.

Foreword

*T*he *Prodigal Son: A Story of Deliverance from Sin* is a candid account of the author's childhood and adult struggles with his identity and sexuality. In his book, life is not a fairy tale and it is not always portrayed as a perfect family.

The Simms were a Christian family with values and morals they expected their children to follow. Many times our children may not live up to our expectations, and the author was no exception.

Harold was the prodigal who strayed and fell into the sin of homosexuality. This book will tell of his journey back to God. It was obvious that He was ashamed of this detestable sin.

This author was set free and delivered from the sin of homosexuality over thirty years ago. You too can be delivered and happy. However, Jesus is the only way.

I'm proud to be married to this author for seven-teen years and counting. He is a wonderful man of God, my friend and my Soulmate. We have come to know God as a deliverer.

I hope you enjoy reading *The Prodigal Son: A Story of Deliverance from Sin* as much as I do.

Mrs. Barbara Simms,
Wife and Best Friend

Chapter 1

The Prodigal Son

The story of the Prodigal Son is found in Luke 15:11-32. Jesus tells His disciples of a son who was lost in the world. This son decided to see what the world had to offer him, so he asks his father to give him his inheritance. The son went out from his father's house to another country and wasted his substance with riotous living. This young man lived an immoral life. He found himself doing things that were beyond his nature; went out and lost everything. He tried to become a citizen of another country. Even though he found himself eating with the swine, he had a praying father. The Bible tells us that the son one day, came to himself.

> "And when he came to himself, he said,
> How many hired servants of my father's
> have bread enough and to spare, and I

perish with hunger! I will arise and go to my father, and will say unto him, Father, I have sinned against heaven, and before thee, And am no more worthy to be called thy son: make me as one of thy hired servants. And he arose, and came to his father. But when he was yet a great way off, his father saw him, and had compassion, and ran, and fell on his neck, and kissed him. And the son said unto him, Father, I have sinned against heaven, and in thy sight, and am no more worthy to be called thy son. But the father said to his servants, Bring forth the best robe, and put it on him; and put a ring on his hand, and shoes on his feet: And bring hither the fatted calf, and kill it; and let us eat, and be merry: For this my son was dead, and is alive again; he was lost, and is found. And they began to be merry."

Luke 15:17-24 (KJV)

Now that is Love! The son repented and asked his father's forgiveness. He was restored to be what he was meant to be. We were all made in the image of God:

"And God said, Let us make man in our image, after our likeness: and let them have dominion over the fish of the sea, and over the fowl of the air, and over the cattle, and over all the earth, and over every creeping thing that creepeth upon the earth. So God created man in his own image, in the image of God created he him; male and female created he them. And God blessed them, and God said unto them, Be fruitful, and multiply, and replenish the earth, and subdue it: and have dominion over the fish of the sea, and over the fowl of the air, and over every living thing that moveth upon the earth." Genesis 1:26-28 (KJV)

Every man and woman was born a sinner. Psalm 51:5 KJV says, "Behold, I was shaped in iniquity; and in sin did my mother conceive me." Genesis, Chapter 3 records that when sin entered the world, all humanity fell. What is sin?

Sin is revolt against the holiness and sovereign will of God. Therefore, it is both a condition of the heart, the mind, the will and affections. (Isa 29:13; Jer 17:9) It is the practical outworking of the condition in thoughts, words and deeds that offend God and transgress His Holy law. (Gen 6:5; Isa 59:12-13)

Sin is in the human heart (Mark 7:20-23). Sin is revealed by the law of God, but it is only as the Holy Spirit enlightens the mind that a person truly sees what righteousness demands of us (Roman 3:20). The origin of sin can be traced back to the first human beings, Adam and Eve, and to their revolt against the Lord."

NIV Compact Dictionary of the Bible. J.D. Douglas & Merrill C. Tenney

A loving God one day redeemed me from the dark world of sin that I chose to take part in out of ignorance. Let us not be so quick to blame everything on the Devil. In St. John 10:10, Jesus explains to us that The thief cometh not, but for to steal, and to kill, and to destroy: I am come that they might have life, and that they might have it more abundantly. Jesus continued on to say: "I am the good shepherd; and the good shepherd giveth His life for the sheep".

You may have seen me with a smiling face and thought I was ever so happy. However, on the inside I was a mess. I was in lost in darkness; I was rebelling against God. Yes, I loved the Lord, but in my mind I wanted Him to accept the life I chose to live. God will not compromise with anyone. We can cry all night long, and attend church every Sunday, but nothing will move God until there is true repentance. Psalms 51:16-17 is a heartfelt prayer from David when he sinned against God: "for thou desires not sacrifice; else would I give it; thou delight not in burnt offering. The sacrifices of God are a broken spirit; a broken and a contrite heart, O God, thou wilt not despise".

My life was at stake, and I had to make a choice. Either I was going to receive Christ as my personal Savior or live in direct disobedience to Him and His Word. One day I opened up and allowed Him into my life. I am so glad He received me just as I was. As God began to restore me back into the man I was created to be, I realized there was no love like the love of God. Some only know the Lord through the eyes of other's, but I was given the chance to know Him for myself.

In the Bible, the Pharisees hated Jesus and showed no compassion, but Jesus said He desired mercy. Even though some want to pronounce judgment on others, the Lord is all about compassion. For sure as you are living and breathing, you have a chance to be restored like I was. He loves you, but He does not tolerate sin. Out of all the things I had done, God was still ready to forgive me. Lord, thank You!

The Lord loves us so much, in Jeremiah 29:11-14 He gave us a promise:

> For I know the thoughts that I think toward you. Saith the Lord, thoughts of peace, and not of evil, to give you an expected end. Then shell ye call upon men, and ye shall go and pray unto me, and I will hearken unto you. And ye shall see me, and find me, when ye shell search for me with all your heart. And I will be found of you, saith the Lord. And I will turn away your captivity, and I will gather you from all the nations, and from all the places whither I have driven you, saith the Lord; and I will bring you again into the place whence I caused you to be carried away captive.

Chapter 2

In the Beginning

———— ❖ ————

My mother Mary, was originally from the state of Mississippi. She was a young unwed mother but sent to Tacoma, Washington to give birth to me in July of 1952. She was unable to care for me so I was placed up for adoption.

I never got to know my biological mother, but was grateful she wanted the best for me. For the next sixty-two years of my life, the Lord had a plan for me. Within that plan, I was faced with and I conquered many storms. In the Bible, Romans 8:37 states, "Nay, in all these things we are more than conquerors through him that loved us."

At the age of two-years-old, I was adopted by a middle-aged Christian couple named Mr. and Mrs. Harold J. Simms, Sr. My birth name was Gilbert. However, as I got older my parents told me that I changed my name to Harold J. Simms before the legal process.

My parents adopted five more children, of which I was the oldest. In 1985 my Sister Betty who was two years younger than me, passed away. Therefore, as of this date, there are four remaining siblings and we are still very close.

We were in church every Sunday as a family. We attended God's Pentecostal Church in Tacoma, Washington, where I now reside as Pastor. This very church is the third oldest African American church in the city of Tacoma (est. 1925). My parents joined the church in 1951.

As a child, I never complained about going to church, I actually enjoyed everything about it. All of the singing, dancing and praising in the spirit was always so interesting to me. It was always such an excitement to spend time with the other children my age. We were all so very close as if we were biological brothers and sisters.

Today, some of those same children are now serving as local Bishops, Pastors, Evangelists and other ministry leaders.

Growing up as a child, my mother made sure we knew what the "plan of salvation" meant. One thing she said and I will never forget, "Baby, if you don't get saved, you will go to hell." Well, I needed to know more about "Hell".

Our Mother made sure we understood what Heaven was and what Hell meant. The Bibles says in Proverbs 22:6 says: "Train up a child in the way he should go: and when he is old, he will not depart form it." My parents wanted us to know the truth, and the consequences of not following the truth.

I can appreciate how they exercised Matthew 19:14 where it says, "Jesus said, suffer little children, and forbid them not, to come unto me: for of such is the kingdom of Heaven." They made sure we knew who Jesus was. Glory to God!

Chapter 3

Receiving Jesus Christ as a Child

Our Annual State meeting always convened in the month of January and held at the God's Pentecostal Church in Tacoma, Washington. You could definitely feel the presence of God and it was an experience neither I or my family will ever forget. One night the presence of God was so strong, I found myself on the floor crying out to God. That night, even my parents were in tears while my three year-old sister Betty, was not quite understanding. All I know is that a change had come over me! At 6 years old, I knew I was saved: born again because of His love for me.

On our way home from church everyone in the car was quiet. Finally my Mother asked me what happened tonight. My response to her was that I received Jesus Christ as my Lord and Savior. The reason I know this is because, "He tickled my heart". That response made my parents want to laugh because I was a child and I gave them a child-like answer.

As time went on, my parents began to see a change in my life. Even though I was still a child, they could see a level of maturity, especially in the things I chose to do and not do. I was getting very serious about being saved.

My parents knew there was a calling on my life. The Lord ministered to my mother through a dream. After praying and searching the scriptures related to her dream, she was led to read I Samuel 1:11 which says, "And she vowed a vow, and said O Lord of hosts, if thou wilt indeed look on the affliction of thine handmaid, but wilt give unto thin handmaid a man child, then I will give him unto the Lord all the days of his life." This is the Word that supports the dream my mother had concerning me.

Never doubt your child's salvation and never tell them they are too young to do anything for the Lord. When they receive Christ, they are ready to live for Christ!

As your child grows and goes through life, they are going to be faced with real challenges. The Bible says those who live Godly will suffer persecution. Man, Woman, Boy and Girl, no one is exempt. Keep praying over your child as they grow. Even though my life took a turn, my Parents still loved me; they kept on praying for me.

Satan had a plan to destroy my life and he is seeking to destroy the children in this generation. If the parents who are living an alternative lifestyle continue to introduce their children to this, they are giving Satan complete access to them every day. Dear Parents, be wise and alert. Your children must be brought up in the way that pleases God!

Chapter 4

The Warfare Is On

W hen you accept the Lord into your life, the spiritual warfare is on. The Word says in Ephesians 6:10-12 KJV: "Finally, my brethren, be strong in the Lord, and in the power of his might. Put on the whole armor of God that ye may be able to stand against the wiles of the devil. For we wrestle not against flesh and blood, but against principalities, against powers, against the rulers of the darkness of this world, against spiritual wickedness in the high places.

Today I pray for our children everywhere. Satan is no respecter of person. It saddens me that Prayer has been taken out of our schools, and those that practice homosexuality are raising our children. There are so many influences in our society today that is attempting to lure our children away from God. However, he can be defeated if we take the time and cover them in prayer. Remember the spirit of Satan got into King

Herod. Matthew 2:13 NIV says: "When they had gone, an angel of the Lord appeared to Joseph in a dream. Get up he said, 'Take the child and his mother and escape to Egypt. Stay there until I tell you, for Herod is going to search for the child to kill him.' " We must pray for our children's minds and souls.

It was discovered in first grade that I was being considered as a slow learner. In results of testing, it was determined I had a learning disability and brain damage . Since I was adopted, it was suggested that I be given back to the state. A school for mentally ill children was being considered. However, my parents said no. They were Christians and always told me that I can do all things through Christ Jesus. The school system placed me in a "special class." In this class there were children who had serious mental challenges. I did not learn anything while I there.

For at least six years, my parents taught me to read and write at home. When I entered junior high school, they lobbied for me to be put in a regular class. Thanks be to the Lord, I did well. From the time I got into the 8th grade, I made the honor roll up until high school. After that, I graduated with honors from Mount Tahoma in 1971. My parents encouraged me to apply for college, but fear attached to my mind. I knew my school records would follow me including reports of being a slower learner. I took the LST test and did well. Being accepted at the University of Washington in Seattle gave me great joy. It was a fight, but I won by the help of God. I received my B.A. in Political Science, and later I received my Master's Degree in Bible Studies. God extended His favor to me.

It is a fact that if God is for us, who can be against us? We are more than conquerors through Him that loved us! It was a fight, but I won!

Chapter 5

The Introduction to Homosexuality

A Child's Nightmare

Our children are vulnerable and we must continue to pray a covering over them. Even when Satan tries attacking them, we as born again believers have the power of the Holy Spirit to combat any spirit. Jesus said: "Then were there brought unto him little children that he should put his hands on them, and pray: and the disciples rebuked them. But Jesus said, Suffer little children, and forbid them not, to come unto me: for of such is the kingdom of heaven." (Matthew 19:13-14 KJV).

One outstanding story in the Bible tells of a woman whose daughter had an unclean spirit.

> For a certain woman, whose young daughter had an unclean spirit, heard of

him, and came and fell at his feet: The
woman was a Greek, a Syrophenician
by nation; and she besought him that
he would cast forth the devil out of her
daughter. But Jesus said unto her, Let
the children first be filled: for it is not
meet to take the children's bread, and to
cast it unto the dogs. And she answered
and said unto him, Yes, Lord: yet the
dogs under the table eat of the children's
crumbs. And he said unto her, For this
saying go thy way; the devil is gone out
of thy daughter. (Mark 7:25-29 KJV)

In this text, Jesus was not saying this woman was
a dog. Regardless of her race and religion nothing
kept her from coming to Jesus for the healing of her
daughter. Faith in her Lord, made her whole. Scripture
does not say what this unclean spirit was, and it does
not matter. The child was healed and delivered. Another
parent brought their son to Jesus who had a tormenting
spirit. This spirit had tormented this young man since
childhood. The parent had brought the young man to
the disciples, but the disciples could not cast out the
evil spirit because of their lack of faith. The Word
says: "And they brought him unto him: and when he
saw him, straightway the spirit tare him; and he fell on

the ground, and wallowed foaming. And he asked his father, How long is it ago since this came unto him? And he said, Of a child. And ofttimes it hath cast him into the fire, and into the waters, to destroy him: but if thou canst do any thing, have compassion on us, and help us. " (Mark 9:20-22 KJV).

Don't give up on your child because of a behavioral pattern you witness. I am grateful for the prayers of the saints, but most importantly the Prayers of my Parents. They did not give up on me.

At the age of Seven, I was molested again by an older child. He was twice my age. This went on for about five years. He would present me with gifts to keep me quiet and made me believe that I would go to jail if I told anyone. I was bound by fear and intimidation. Years after this abuse, I finally told my parents. They were hurt by the news.

If you are a parent, assure your child that they can come to you about anything at any time and if anyone touches them inappropriately, they should say something. Don't hold on to it for years like I did.

While I was in elementary school, kids would call me sissy and would say, "You act like a girl." Those remarks bothered me, but I never questioned who I was. The principal and I had a very comforting conversation. He stated that I didn't have nothing to worry because I was not a homosexual. Even though I didn't fully understand that word, it still brought me comfort. Proverbs 18:21 says, "Death and life are in the power of the tongue; and they that love it shall eat the fruit thereof." This principal was kind and did not curse me with observation of my behavior.

Be mindful of how you label your child because of their behavior. My parents and family extended grace to me. Even though they may have had some wonders, they never voiced their concern. However, they continued to pray for me. The Principal could have sided with the other child, but that didn't happen.

Yes, I did play with girls a lot. I was very close to my sister Betty and had some obvious feminine characteristics, but that was all.

My prayer and heart goes out for the children who are introduced to homosexuality and have to subject themselves to people with this type of spirit and behavior. My prayer is they accept who God made them to be, and not what this corrupt society says they should be.

God says:

> And God said let us make man in our image after our likeness; and let them have dominion over the fish of the sea, and over the fowl of the air and over

the cattle, and over all the earth, and over every creeping thing that creepeth upon the earth. So God created man in his own image, in the image of God created he him; male and female created he them. And God blessed them. And God said unto them, be fruitful and multiply, and replenish the earth, and subdue it and dominion over the fish of the sea, and over the fowl of the air, and over every living thing that moved upon the earth (Genesis 1:26-28 KJV).

Let us pray for the children who are in the household of parents who practice this lifestyle. Pray that they will not choose any of their ways. Let us also pray that their parents will repent and allow the Lord to change them to His image. God loves homosexuals; but He hates the sin, the act. Look what He did for me!

I Corinthians 6:9 NIV says:

Do you not know that the wicked will not inherit the kingdom of God? Do not be deceived: neither the sexual immoral nor idolaters nor adulterers nor male prostitutes nor homosexual offenders

nor thieves nor the greedy nor drunkards nor slanderers nor swindlers will
inherit the kingdom of God and that is
what some of you were. But you were
washed; you were sanctified, and were
justified in the name of the Lord Jesus
Christ and by the spirit of our God.

Chapter 6

Living In The Closet

How do you define homosexuality? Homosexuality for me was a deep place of darkness. Being led by my feelings and emotions, I opened up a very dark door. I chose to walk through that door and close it behind me. For fifteen years, I experienced a lifestyle that was not of my morals and righteous living. I felt like I was trapped and did not know how to find my way out.

In the fall of 1971, I had been accepted into the University of Washington. That same year I graduated from Mount Tahoma High School. I lived on campus, so this was my first time being away from home. Even though it was a bittersweet place for me, my parents were very happy I was attending, especially considering the many challenges I faced while in school.

While on campus, I wanted to take part in some activities. I ended up attending a meeting that brought back painful memories of my childhood. I could not get the meeting out of my mind. I started questioning myself. *Am I a homosexual?* I went back to the meeting and chose to begin a friendship with this group. I did not realize I was becoming reattached to something that was not honorable to God.

My first sexual experience as an adult was at the age of nine-teen with a man. My flesh and emotions became attached. Even though I told myself I would not do it again, my mind kept going back to the man I had a sexual encounter with. I would go home every weekend to attend church because I knew that is where I belong. Yes, I was guilty and I knew I was trapped in this. The Apostle Paul said in Romans 7:24 (NIV): "What a wretched man I am who will rescue me from this body of death" (Romans 7:24 NIV). Those were my same thoughts!

After I graduated from college in 1977, I decided not to attend graduate school. My parents were getting older, so I went to work. Going out to the bars at night drove me deeper into that dark place, because I found myself having encounters with different men every night.

When I got up to go to church, the Word of God would convict me, but I was trapped! There is no such thing as "I am doing this because someone molested me." I had no self control, no self-worth or respect for myself.

Because I did not want to disrespect or disappoint my mother, I met a guy and moved out. While I continued to take care of my parents, my Mother would preach to me everyday; I listened and I cried. She did what any other Godly Mother would do and that was tell me the truth. After all of that, my life with my partner did not work out.

In 1985, something happened! I was 32 years-old and my way of living began to get old. Both my father and my Sister Betty had passed away. My mother was in her eighties. I loved God, loved church and I was ready to get out of my mess. I only knew about the do's and don'ts of religion. However, I did not experience the real Grace of God until I surrendered and said "Yes" to Him.

Chapter 7

Out of the Closet

The Process of Returning to the Lord

W hen the Prodigal son came to himself, he was eating with the swine. The Bible says in Luke 15:14-18 (KJV), "And when he had spent all, there arose a mighty famine in that land; and he began to be in want. And he went and joined himself to a citizen of that country; and he sent him into his fields to feed swine. And he would fain have filled his belly with the husks that the swine did eat: and no man gave unto him. And when he came to himself, he said, How many hired servants of my father's have bread enough and to spare, and I perish with hunger! I will arise and go to my father, and will say unto him, Father, I have sinned against heaven, and before thee."

Going to church every Sunday and feeling sorry for myself was not enough. I was bound and ashamed of this lifestyle. Being raised in a Christian home and being taught the Word, I knew there was a way out. The way out was through the Lord and Savior Jesus Christ. However, I just did not know how to get there. There were a few people who could not deal with what I was going through, and in their minds I was bound for hell. However, as the scripture says, I cried unto the Lord, and He heard me! Thank You God, for hearing me!

The Process Begins

On December 31, 1985, my cousin Joann and I were getting ready to go out to one of the local clubs in Tacoma. All of our lives we spent New Year's Eve night in church, but this night we had been smoking weed and were ready to party and have a good time. Not sure what came over my cousin that night but she wanted to go to church before we went to the club. I agreed to go as long as we were still planning on partying afterwards.

Off to church we go! My own mother was the pastor at that time. As the Word of God was being preached, I began to feel a need to surrender my life. My intoxication and highness was slowly diminishing. I could hear my inner-man crying *"Out, Lord! Help me, I want out."* At 11:50 pm, an altar call was made. My cousin Joann and I found ourselves on the altar, repenting and giving our lives back to God!

Acts 4:12 KJV says: "Neither is there salvation in any other; for there is none other name under heaven given among men, whereby we must be saved." If you call, God will answer. Zechariah 13:9 KJV says: "They shall call on my name, and I will hear them: I will say, it is my people: and they shall say, the Lord is my God." Without a doubt, the Lord saved us!

I felt like the woman who was caught in the act of adultery. Jesus told her in John 8:11, "Go and sin no more." We left the church rejoicing the Lord. Now, we begin the process of becoming like Christ.

Chapter 8

Tell Me the Truth

As I continued to walk through this deliverance process, I struggled with deep feelings. Living this lifestyle for fifteen years there was definitely a stronghold on my mind. I struggled with longing for my partner and my friends. Warfare existed! The battle of the mind existed! Everytime I revisit these places, a strong conviction would come upon me and I would repent. Even though I was forgiven and I was saved, the struggle to do the right thing was there. I am reminded of what the Apostle Paul said in Romans 7:24 NIV: "What a wretched man I am! Who will rescue me from this body of death?"

There were times when I felt like giving up. I was too afraid to talk to anyone at my church. However, I needed someone to tell me the truth. I decided to seek out a Pastor in hopes that He would share truth with me. Because of my upbringing and being taught the way of holiness, I didn't get the strong advice I needed. I was told what my flesh wanted to hear. Anytime you hear something that satisfies the flesh, it may not always be what you need. St. John 8:32 says, "Ye shall know the truth, and the truth shall make you free. " The advice I received, did not set me free. I Corinthians 2:15 says: "The spiritual man makes judgments about all things. But he himself is not subject to any mans judgment."

Pastors have been called, appointed and are responsible for people's spiritual life. It was disappointing to hear what this pastor had to say, because I reached out to him for help. This was a conversation I had twenty-eight years ago. Today, believe it or not, there are so many people who are still bound because they are not hearing the truth about the sin of homosexuality. Instead, those that practice this lifestyle are still in the choir, still playing musical instruments and are still allowed to lead worship services. Are these men and women being taught the truth according to the Word?

It's the Word that will draw them. Joshua 7:11 says: "Israel has sinned, they have violated my covenant which I commanded them to keep."

My prayer is that all Pastors would take heed and do things according to the Word of God. Ezekiel 3:18-19 says, "When I say to a wicked man, you will surely die, and you do not warn him or speak out to dissuade him from his evil ways in order to save his life, that wicked man will die for his sin and I will hold you accountable for his blood. But if you warn the wicked man and he does not turn form his wickedness or from his evil ways, he will die for his sin; but you will have save yourself." As a Pastor, if we refuse to speak the truth, their blood will be on our hands.

Thank God for His grace and mercy. God led me to an Evangelist at my church. She has known me most of my life. I was ever so ready to hear and receive the truth. I was tired of grieving the Holy Ghost and I wanted to be healed for real. Just like the Women in the 9th chapter of Matthew, I was determined to be completely delivered that night. This Evangelist began to pray and speak with power and authority over my life that night.

Out of all the sexual encounters I've had, I wanted to get tested. Praise God, I did not contract the virus! It is and was by God's grace that He kept me.

Chapter 9

The Power of God's Love

S in is what separates us from God. If we repent of our sins, the Lord will forgive us of all unrighteousness. 1 John 1:5-10 says:

> "This then is the message which we have heard of him and declare unto you, that God is light, and in him is no darkness at all. If we say that we have fellowship with him, and walk in darkness, we lie, and do not the truth; but if we walk in the light, as he is in the light, we have fellowship one with another and the blood of Jesus Christ his Son cleanseth us from all sin. If we way that we have no sin, we deceive ourselves, and the truth is not in us. If we confess our sins, he is faithful and just to forgive

us our sins, and to cleanse us from all unrighteousness. If we say that we have not sinned, we make him a liar, and his word is not in us."

You can not justify your feelings or your sin by the Word of God. I recall trying connect with those who called themselves "Christian and Gay". It sounded good and sounded like I could possibly fit into this. However, I still had no peace and I was only hurting and deceiving myself.

These are the last days; God wants to save the lost. The bible says in Galatians 5:19-21 (KJV):

"Now the works of the flesh are manifest, which are these: "Adultery, fornication, uncleanness, lasciviousness, idolatry, witchcraft, hatred, variance, emulations wrath, strife, seditions heresies, envying, murders drunkenness, reveling, and such like; of the which I tell you before, as I have also told you in time past, that they which do such things shall not inherit the kingdom of God."

It is the Lord's desire to save us, but we must be willing to repent of our wrong. The key word is repent! Isaiah 1:18-20 says,

> "Come now, and let us reason together, saith the Lord: though your sins be as scarlet, they shall be as white as snow; though they be red like crimson, they shall be as wool. If ye be willing and obedient, ye shall eat the good of the land: But if ye refuse and rebel, ye shall be devoured with the sword: for the mouth of the Lord hath spoken it. "

There is forgiveness through Jesus Christ. His blood will wash away our sin. There is no such thing as being born a homosexual or God made a mistake about your gender. It clearly states in Genesis 1:26-28 (KJV):

> "And God said, Let us make man in our image, after our likeness: and let them have dominion over the fish of the sea, and over the fowl of the air, and over the cattle, and over all the earth, and over every creeping thing that creepeth upon the earth. So God created man in his own image, in the image of God

33

> created he him; male and female cre-
> ated he them. And God blessed them,
> and God said unto them, Be fruitful,
> and multiply, and replenish the earth,
> and subdue it: and have dominion over
> the fish of the sea, and over the fowl of
> the air, and over every living thing that
> moveth upon the earth."

Be not confused! God did not make a mistake with your gender. If you were born a male, that's what you are! If you were born a female, that's what you are. You were made in the image of God. Satan is a full time deceiver. Know the truth and be free!

The Corinthians church had homosexuality in their church. Paul preached the Word of God to them. In I Corinthians 5:1-6 it says, "It is reported commonly that there is fornication among you and such fornica-tion as is not so much as named among the Gentiles that one should have his fathers wife. Your glorying is not good known ye not that a little leaven leavened the whole lump?"

The behavior of this church are like many in our churches today. I Corinthians 6:9-11 says, "Know ye not that the unrighteous shall not inherit the Kingdom of God? Be not deceived: neither fornicators, nor idol-aters, nor adulterers, nor effeminate, nor abusers of themselves with mankind, Nor thieves, nor covetous, nor drunkards, nor revilers, nor extortioners, shall inherit the kingdom of God. And such were some of you: but ye are washed, but ye are sanctified, but ye are justified in the name of the Lord Jesus, and by the Spirit of our God."

Chapter 10

Heaven and Hell

In the book of Revelation 20:10-15, it says:

"And the devil that deceived them was cast into the lake of fire and brimstone, where the beast and the false prophet are, and shall be tormented day and night forever and ever. And I saw a great white throne, and him that sat on it, from whose face the earth and the heaven fled away; and there was found no place for them. And I saw the dead, small and great, stand before God; and the books were opened: and another book was opened, which is the book of life: and the dead were judged out of those things which were written in the books, according to their works. And the sea gave up the dead which were in it; and death and hell delivered up the dead which were in them: and they were judged every man according to their works. And death and hell were cast into the lake of fire. This is the second death.

And whosoever was not found written in the book of life was cast into the lake of fire."

All of my life I have been told that Hell is real. As a child I was taught the difference between Heaven and Hell. Hell is definitely where I choose not to spend eternity. All through-out the scriptures, it's been made clear that Heaven is where God desires His people.

Revelation 21:1-4 KJV says: "And I saw a new heaven and a new earth: for the first heaven and the first earth were passed away; and there was no more sea. And I John saw the holy city, new Jerusalem, coming down from God out of heaven, prepared as a bride adorned for her husband. And I heard a great voice out of heaven saying, Behold, the tabernacle of God is with men, and he will dwell with them, and they shall be his people, and God himself shall be with them, and be their God. And God shall wipe away all tears from their eyes; and there shall be no more death, neither sorrow, nor crying, neither shall there be any more pain: for the former things are passed away."

It is a fact that when you receive Christ into your life, Heaven will be your home when you leave this Earth. Heaven will be our final destination! Praise God!

Chapter 11

Life As An Overcomer

M y parents were excellent role models when it
came to having a successful marriage. They
were blessed and, in my eyes, their marriage was perfect. For me, marriage or the subject of marriage has
never been a subject of mine. However, I've always
observed how my Father complimented my mother,
and she did the same as well. Because of my past, I
never thought the institution of marriage was for me.
However, because I have now been born again, as the
scripture says, all things have become new. Praise God!

Twenty-five years ago, I started searching for my
biological parents. My adoptive parents had always
encouraged me to keep searching for them. Even as
crazy as it may sound, I believe it was God's Divine
plan that they put me up for adoption.

In my massive search from Jackson, Mississippi to
Tacoma Washington, I received a letter from a lady by

the name of Ms. Barbara Duckworth. The dear Sister agreed to pray with me in my search. Barbara and I began corresponding by telephone and letters and by email. At the end our conversation we would sometimes end it with prayer.

For whatever reason, I felt very comfortable with sharing my past life experiences and deliverance with this dear sister. The more we talked, the more freer I felt. Yes, old things really do pass away, according to II Cornthians 5:17. The adversary desires to keep you bound, but God's Word will set you free!

One thing that began to attract me to this sister was the fact that she never judged me but she listened. Barbara was indeed a friend and I believe God was doing something unique in this friendship.

In 1998, something very strange happened. While I was in church, minding my own business, a minister approaches me and asks if I had been looking for a wife.

Not sure why, but that question did not set well with me and my response to him was not a very pleasant response. Later that month, someone I respected asked me the same question. My first thought was, *who would want somebody like me?* Little did I know, God had a plan.

After several more incidences on this marriage matter kept coming up, I realize I could be blocking one of the greatest blessings in my life. I finally repented and submitted to whatever the will of God is/was for my life.

One important thing we all must remember, it doesn't matter how dark and gray our past may have been, God has to power to give us a very bright and prosperous future! Once I got past all of that, the Lord revealed to me that this dear sister from Jackson Mississippi, Ms. Barbara was my wife. At this point, God was going to have to take it from here, because I didn't know how I was supposed to tell her this. Once again God began to reveal and seal this relationship through conversation.

On April 30, 1999, it was time for me to finally meet this Lady in person. I flew to Jackson, Mississippi. To some it may have seemed like a fast move, but when God is in something – time doesn't mean anything. During the Sunday morning service, at her church, I was asked to bring greetings. That was my God moment and opportunity to ask Barbara to be my wife. With a ring in my hand, kneeling down on one knee, Barbara said yes! It was a moment to behold. God is able to do anything!

On June 3, 2000, Barbara and I became one flesh. We are currently serving as Pastor's together at God's Pentecostal Church in Tacoma, Washington.

Later, because of our obedience, we have witnessed two marriages of our children: Our son, Sabian and his wife Audrey, and our daughter Alicia and her husband Stanley. We are blessed with seven grandchildren. Malachi 3:6 KJV says, "I the Lord do not change". With that being said, God's will and plan concerning marriage will never change.

Marriage was designed for a man and a woman. He will never bless marriage that goes against His plan. The Bible says: "But your iniquities have separated you from your God: your sins have hidden his face from you, so that he will not hear" (Isaiah 59:2 KJV). If you are in a relationship that is not according to scripture, God has given you a way out! Repent!

Chapter 12

The Conclusion of the Matter

Hebrews 9:27 KVJ says: "And as it is appointed unto men once to die but after this the judgement."

One thing for sure, we will all stand before God. Men and Women will be judged by their works. This is the whole truth according to the Word of God. Ecclesiastes 11:13 KJV says, "Let us hear the conclusion of the whole matter: Fear God, and keep his commandments: for this is the whole duty of man. For God shall bring every work into judgment, with every secret thing, whether it be good, or whether it be evil." The Word also says, in Revelation 20:11-14 KJV:

> "And I saw a great white throne, and him
> that sat on it, from whose face the earth
> and the heaven fled away; and there was
> found no place for them. And I saw the

dead, small and great, stand before God; and the books were opened: and another book was opened, which is the book of life: and the dead were judged out of those things which were written in the books, according to their works. And the sea gave up the dead which were in it; and death and hell delivered up the dead which were in them: and they were judged every man according to their works. And death and hell were cast into the lake of fire. This is the second death."

If you were born a man, you will stand as a man before God, and if you were born a woman, you will stand as a woman. God will not honor what you thought you felt or thought you wanted to be. If you think God has made a mistake, you have been deceived. It is God's law that will judge those who refuses to accept Him. Those who have made Christ their choice will receive mercy according to St. John 3:16. It reads as follows: "For God so loved the world, that he gave his only begotten Son, that whosoever believeth in him should not perish, but have everlasting life. For God sent not his Son into the world to condemn the world; but that the world through him might be saved. He that belie-veth on him is not condemned: but he that believeth not is condemned already, because he hath not believed in the name of the only begotten Son of God."

It is a fact that the unrighteous shall not in inherit the kingdom of God. Don't let this be you!

This is not about religion, this is God's truth. You and I will one day die. None of the laws that man has adopted will stand before God almighty, only what is written in the Bible. However, if you have received Christ in your life you will be saved from the curse of the law.

Hell does not have to be your final resting place if you turn from rebellion and disbelief. You make the choice. God loves you.

In Romans 8:1-11 KJV, this is what the Word says concerning you:

> "There is therefore now no condemnation to them which are in Christ Jesus, who walk not after the flesh, but after the Spirit. For the law of the Spirit of life in Christ Jesus hath made me free from the law of sin and death. For what the law could not do, in that it was weak through the flesh, God sending his own Son in the likeness of sinful flesh, and for sin, condemned sin in the flesh: That

the righteousness of the law might be fulfilled in us, who walk not after the flesh, but after the Spirit. For they that are after the flesh do mind the things of the flesh; but they that are after the Spirit the things of the Spirit. For to be carnally minded is death; but to be spiritually minded is life and peace. Because the carnal mind is enmity against God: for it is not subject to the law of God, neither indeed can be. So then they that are in the flesh cannot please God. But ye are not in the flesh, but in the Spirit, if so be that the Spirit of God dwell in you. Now if any man have not the Spirit of Christ, he is none of his. And if Christ be in you, the body is dead because of sin; but the Spirit is life because of righteousness. But if the Spirit of him that raised up Jesus from the dead dwell in you, he that raised up Christ from the dead shall also quicken your mortal bodies by his Spirit that dwelleth in you..

If you are willing and ready to turn your life around, pray this prayer. Allow the Lord to begin a transformation in you.

"The Sinners Prayer"

Spiritual Warfare Bible NKJV. Kimberly Daniels, Prayers that bring Change, 133-136 (Special Emphasis added by Pastor Harold Simms Jr.)

My dear Lord Jesus, I have made the decision to come out of the lifestyle that I know is an abomination in your sight. Lord, I repent for allowing the wicked desires of my flesh to have rule over me. Lord, I renounce every soul tie of every person that I have lain in sin with. I renounce the perversity of the lifestyle. I declare that I hate it, because I cannot be delivered from what I love. I love the people who are bound in homosexuality, but I hate the lifestyle. It is an abomination before you, Lord. I curse the spirit of witchcraft that comes with this perverted lifestyle. Father, deliver me from the shame and the hurt. Though my flesh experienced demonic pleasure, my soul was always in turmoil. I openly announce that I do not want to live a life of lies anymore. I was created to be MAN/WOMEN. I was beautifully and wonderfully made in the image of God. God is not the author of confusion.

I shut my ear gates to the lies of the enemy that say I was born gay and can never be delivered. I declare, "Once gay is not always gay" I am delivered!!!! The perversities that I once enjoyed and allowed free passage into my mind exist no more. Lord, I repent for going against the natural order of things. I declare the truth of Romans 1, which says that homosexuality/lesbianism is unnatural. I cast down every imagination of this lifestyle that tries to exalt itself over the knowledge of God. I understand that Your Son, Jesus took on all my sins of homosexuality/lesbianism on the cross, and I am redeemed. Lord, I renounce everything that I participated in that seeded my soul. I renounce gay pride and every sign and symbol of the lifestyle. I come against that vision of the rainbow that represented a covenant between the devil and me. I renounce the language that I spoke pertaining to his lifestyle. Lord, I repent for lusting after the same sex, fantasizing about the same sex, and engaging in any behavior with the same sex that is considered an abomination in your sight. Lord, I repent for setting my affections on the things of this earth instead of things above. I repent for putting creation before my creator. I plead the blood of Jesus over my mind, and thank you for not allowing me to be turned over to reprobation. I want to be fully delivered and my mind renewed. I know it is a process. Take me from level to level and glory to glory. I already have the VICTORY! Lord, allow me to become an advocate to cry out loudly against the homosexual agenda and its plans so that other men and women can be free indeed.

I declare that my body is the temple of the living God. I cast down every perverted spirit that exists in me. I now that

Jeremiah 17:9 says, "The heart is deceitful above all thing," and I do not trust my heart – I trust Jesus!! God knew what He was doing when He created me!! All old things are passed away; I am a new creature in Jesus' name. Amen and Amen.

References

All scriptures were from the:

The Original Thompson Chain Reference Study Bible
Fourth improved edition updated

The Sinner's Prayer was submitted from the:
Spiritual Warfare Bible NKJV New King James Version

Highly Recommended Documentary on Deliverance:
Such Were Some of You.

A critical resource for: Pastors, Ministry Leaders,
Teachers and Families.

Mastering Life Ministries
P.O. Box 770
Franklin, TN 37065
(615) 507-4166

CPSIA information can be obtained
at www.ICGtesting.com
Printed in the USA
JSHW010710280323
39539JS00004B/29